THE CAT THAT CHANGED MY LIFE

50 CATS TALK CANDIDLY
ABOUT HOW THEY BECAME WHO THEY ARE

BRUCE ERIC KAPLAN

SIMON & SCHUSTER

New York   London   Toronto   Sydney

SIMON & SCHUSTER
Rockefeller Center
1230 Avenue of the Americas
New York, NY 10020

First Simon & Schuster trade paperback edition 2004

SIMON & SCHUSTER and colophon are registered trademarks of
Simon & Schuster, Inc.

For information about special discounts for bulk purchases,
please contact Simon & Schuster Special Sales:
1-800-456-6798 or business@simonandschuster.com.

Designed by Chris Welch
Manufactured in the United States of America

1   3   5   7   9   10   8   6   4   2

The Library of Congress has cataloged the hardcover edition
as follows:
Kaplan, Bruce Eric.
The cat that changed my life : 50 cats talk candidly about how they
became who they are / Bruce Eric Kaplan.
p. cm.
1. Cats—Fiction. 2. Cats—Pictorial works. I. Title.
PS3561.A5534 C38 2001
813'.6—dc21   2002023878

ISBN 0-7432-1944-9

0-7432-5785-5 (Pbk)

FOR KATE,
WHO FELL OUT OF A TREE

INTRODUCTION

Change is good, or at least I have heard people say that. But what I have never understood is, when things change for the worse, why is that good? Here's another expression—the more things change, the more they stay the same. That makes sense, yet . . . if it's true, how do you explain the vast difference between a grape and a raisin? And while we are on the topic, I think if someone asks you for spare change, he or she doesn't really want coins at all. Instead, I believe their subconscious is asking you to help them become something else. But I've noticed that the person gets frustrated when you try to tell him or her this, so I could be wrong.

What you are about to read is an exploration of the nature of change. I devoted four years of my life to traveling across the country (okay, mostly I stayed in and around New Jersey, but periodically I left the metropolitan area) asking cats who was the individual in their life that had changed them the most and why. I conducted over forty thousand interviews and then winnowed them down to the fifty most interesting responses.

I sketched each cat as I spoke with him or her. I feel this helped me get particularly intimate answers to my questions. A unique energy is created between the artist and the subject. Each time one looks up from the paper, it is with a deeper understanding, and the subject can't help but sense this (that is, unless the subject smells a mouse in the nearby vicinity, in which case the subject needs to find it before it can really concentrate). A rhythm is created between the two individuals, and the veil the subject normally wears is slowly dropped, until he or she is virtually bare.

"Change" is such a nebulous word. Actually, all words are nebulous, even the word "nebulous" (depending on how you use it). But the point is, there was a wild disparity in the answers to my simple question. Some of the cats, such as Claude, spoke of another cat that had passed on a meaningful personal philosophy. Others—for example, Bones—described a cat that did something terrible that forever scarred them. And then there were those such as Moo-Moo who spoke of a cat whose warmth and goodness had nurtured their own self-improvement.

Of course, there was a lot of talk of love. *L'amour, l'amour, toujours l'amour* (or something to that effect). But the illicit passion that changed Knickers's life is vastly different from the obsessive love that changed Haggie's life. And as you will see, some (like Bumpers) never mention the word "love," yet I suspect love lies at the heart of their answers, even if they have no idea that it does. But that often seems true of all of us. We talk about a million different things, yet really it's always just about love (and guilt, obviously). Speaking of which, there is a lot of guilt in these pages, most notably from Peaches and Hildegarde. And yet, like love, each story of guilt is different in its own way.

At the same time, there are some striking similarities between the cats in this collection. Most notably, two come to my mind. One is that, overall, they are a highly sensitive and introspective group. This is their reputation, of course, but I had no idea of their level of sensitivity until I began this project. Take Brownie, for example. A cat said one simple thing to him and from that moment on, nothing in his life was the same again. Kip and Cecil tell equally distressing stories. One could say that they perhaps overreacted in these situations. But being somewhat sensitive myself, it is hard for me to say that they are overly so.

The second similarity is almost amusing (but sadly, like so many things in life, not quite). All these cats lead exciting and varied lives wholly independent of the human race. Again, maybe that's obvious just by looking at the species, but when you read these testimonies, it becomes horrifyingly apparent. I suppose there could be a case made that it is denial on some of these cats' parts, but I have to tell you, I don't think that's it. I just think that their own kind are much more interesting to them. And who can blame them? I never encountered a person who was half as interesting as a cat. Let's be realistic here— you'll never meet a cat who talks about any kind of mortgage rates and that puts them way ahead of us.

Anyway, on with the book. I hope you like it. And if it changes you in any way, please let me know.

BRUCE ERIC KAPLAN
Los Angeles, California

My parents spent their whole lives lazing around, only occasionally getting up to press their noses against the window, but never actually going out and doing anything. I'm sure I would have ended up like them if I hadn't known Butch.

Butch was a true legend—the ugliest, meanest creature in the neighborhood. The interesting thing was that despite his vile personality, he always seemed to get the most interesting toys, the newest snacks, the longest pieces of string. On top of everything else, he always had the hottest sexual partners—male or female. Day after day, I watched him disappear into the bushes with someone different until finally, one afternoon, I asked him what his secret was. He smiled and said it was simple. When he saw something he wanted, he just grabbed it before anyone else could. He hissed, he clawed, he screamed—he did whatever it took to make sure he got there first.

Ever since that, I've been just like Butch. It's been wild. I've had sex with almost everyone who's ever sauntered by me. I've tasted treats that others only dream about and I've scratched some of the most tactile surfaces that exist, unlike my father, who lies day in and day out on the same smelly pillow.

CLAUDE

Baltimore, Maryland
May 17, 1997

Each day, the loneliness eats away at you. You tell yourself that it's not so bad and that some of us are simply meant to be alone, but you don't quite believe it. That's how I was before Juliet moved in, two doors down. She showed up on my steps one day, pushed me under the crawl space, ravaged me, and I've never been lonely again.

Juliet has given my life a purpose. Sometimes I spend all day curled under her so she can nap more restfully. I don't mind that it is uncomfortable for me and that the next day I have a crick in my neck that just won't go away. I don't even care when she laughs at how I am tilting my head, because I am glad I can bring her joy in some small way.

I like to get her savory things to eat. Once I traveled four miles to scavenge the Dumpster of a specialty-food store. Then when I showed her the morsels I had found, she didn't seem interested. It was my fault. I took too long—I should have run faster.

Occasionally I wish she would not always be in a terrible mood, threatening to leave me at any time. But then I think, if she wasn't exactly who she is, I wouldn't love her as much as I do.

HAMPY
Brookline, Massachusetts
March 31, 2000

Sure, now I seem really confident and secure with who I am, but I used to be a mess—a silly, empty-headed creature who only cared about getting a male's attention. I would sit and lick myself all day long because I thought no one could ever love me if I had any burrs on me or if my fur wasn't completely white.

Then I became friends with Dorothy. She's so totally together, and of course the second she met me, she saw I wasn't. So she invited me to come to her backyard one afternoon to meet some of her friends. She said I should bring a bird or a rat, whatever I could scrounge up. It was a potluck.

When we assembled, Dorothy explained to all of us that we were victims of our culture. From an early age, we had been bombarded with images in calendars and greeting cards and mugs that taught us that we had to be these cute little idiots that never had a real thought, but just looked sweet and cuddly. We cried and shared stories and offered each other support.

That was years ago, but we still meet at least once a week and have all evolved into amazing creatures.

JELLY BEAN
Verona, New Jersey
August 4, 2001

Jinx was never a close friend. She was just an acquaintance I might run into now and then and make small talk with. Once she happened to mention a tree she had heard about that was supposed to have very good bark. We made plans to go see this tree the following week. But then it was drizzly, so we canceled. We made plans to go another day, but then she had some hair-ball situation.

We kept making plans, but for one reason or another, we never got to the tree with the good bark. Then one morning a mutual friend told me that Jinx had been put to sleep the night before.

Shocked and upset, I immediately set off to visit the tree myself. As soon as I saw it in the distance, I began to run. When I got close, I took a leap and jumped onto the trunk, clinging to it like a lunatic. I inhaled deeply, immersing myself in its glorious scent. Then I climbed all over it, rubbing every part of myself against the tree's unique texture. It was an intense experience.

From that day on, I never put off doing anything because I thought, who knows when I could end up like Jinx?

A few years later, I ran into Jinx. She hadn't died. She had just asked our friend to lie to me because she really didn't want to spend time in my company. I made her feel guilty for what she had done, even though on some level I knew that it was because of her lie that I now feel much more alive and fulfilled.

MILTON
White Plains, New York
May 29, 1999

I grew up on a beautiful old farm and had the most perfect existence, but then one morning I was stuck in a cage and taken away to live in my new home—a drab little tract house on a treeless street in a place with stinky air. Now instead of feasting on wonderful country vermin, I was served some manufactured dry food that I was sure was pumped full of chemicals. Instead of running up and down stairs and across fields, I was confined to a grossly carpeted small space.

As the weeks passed, I began to make a list in my head of everything that was wrong with my life. I kept finding things to add, so soon my entire day was spent cataloguing grievances. Finally, one night at dinner, I took a sip of water and it wasn't lukewarm enough. I just grumbled and added it to the enormous list in my head. My housemate, Charles, who was on his last legs at the time, asked what was wrong. I told him at great length how disgusted I was by the water they were serving us.

He took a long look at me and then quietly said, "It's just water." I felt really petty and small. I resolved to stop being whatever it was I was turning into. Through intense behavior modification and meditation, I was able to stop making the list in my head and appreciate what I had in the moment.

BLACKIE

Elizabeth, New Jersey
November 4, 1998

Honey, I wish you could have met my sister Dora. What an amazing character—she basically raised me and I always used to tell her anything good in me came from her. She taught me right from wrong and she always made me feel loved. And on top of everything else, she was fun. No one's fun these days, I don't know why. But where was I? Oh, Dora—you wouldn't believe some of the crazy things she would do.

Once when we were really hungry, she told me to gather dust from under the sofa and chairs and we made dust stew and pretended to eat it. I swear—it made us feel better.

We never had enough heat in the winter and we would shiver to the bone as we tried to sleep. That's when Dora would say it was time to have a day at the races. We would run up and down the hallway. Back then, I thought it was just for fun. But now I know it was to keep us warm.

Dora had an old sock that she named Mary and we would pretend she was our long-lost aunt. How we loved to show Mary all our favorite lounging spots in the apartment.

Dora passed some time ago. I think about her every day. I really want her to be immortalized in some way. We have a distant relative who lives with someone who works in advertising at Miramax. I'm determined to use this connection to get someone to buy the film rights to Dora's story.

FLOPSY

Long Island City, New York
October 22, 2001

It was a stupid, stupid thing to do. Why did I have that brief fling with Henry? I certainly wasn't drawn to him physically. He was constantly smacking his lips—oh, it was so gross. I even asked him why he made that horrible noise (although that's not how I put it). He shrugged and said it was because he loved saltwater taffy, a heavenly substance that sometimes stuck in his mouth. The way he talked about it, I knew I had to try this taffy. And soon I was hooked on it just like he was.

Now I'm an addict. I dumped Henry when his taffy source got dried up. I hooked up with some other creatures that had good connections, until finally I just ended up here on the streets. My whole day is spent trying to dig up taffy. You have no idea how I have to degrade myself to get it.

I've become fat and my teeth are rotten. And I'm always making this noise, trying to loosen the little pieces that stick in my mouth. All I think about day and night is saltwater taffy, so on top of everything else, I have gotten much duller.

PUFFIN
Atlantic City, New Jersey
February 12, 1998

Lucille was a friend of my parents who was in a bad relationship, so she spent a lot of time in our yard.

She was lonely and was of an age where she was starting to feel that she was no longer that attractive. I was young and confused about all the changes my body was going through.

We had a summer of illicit love and then she went back to her mate. I became gay.

KNICKERS

Fair Lawn, New Jersey
November 14, 1999

I had been walking all day long and I was getting tired. I was in a park, and wouldn't you know it, just as I was looking for a patch of sun to lie down in, all I could see were shady spots.

I started to get a chill in my bones. I was desperate for some sun and sleep. Then I saw this perfect spot—only some other creature was already in it. I decided to wait for him to leave.

He saw me waiting for the spot. But he didn't get up. I thought, oh, he just needs a few more minutes. My chill got worse. Well, after about an hour, the bastard still hadn't moved. He looked at me and I knew in that moment that he wasn't moving because I was waiting for that spot.

That was when I truly lost my innocence. I saw the evil that others—complete strangers even—are capable of.

BONES
New York, New York
September 3, 1997

His name was Manuel. He drifted into my driveway one day. He said he was just passing through town and then smiled at me. I smiled back. He had an insouciant quality that I couldn't resist. I gave myself to him and ten minutes later he was gone.

Sixty-five days later, I gave birth to nine little creatures who all look just like him. I have heard that having offspring fulfills you in a way unlike any other. That hasn't happened to me yet. Instead, I despise the little monsters.

I hate Nipsy for being dirty all the time. I hate Hortense for her always having to share something with me. I hate Billy for the way he falls to the ground. I hate Lulu for her dumb expression. I hate Alex for his dumb expression. I hate Sal for bothering me whenever I am trying to defecate. I hate Marnie for her compulsive clawing. I hate Jameson for his pretentiousness. I hate Alice for the way she suddenly twitches.

DOTTIE

West Orange, New Jersey
September 14, 2000

E veryone's afraid of me. I walk by and they say to themselves, stay away from that psychopath, something's wrong with him, just pray he keeps walking.

I don't mind. I've been on my own since I was little and it's made me what I am—a machine who will do anything to survive. I don't have feelings because feelings don't get you shelter or food or even companionship, in my experience.

You live like this for years and you believe that you have a shell around you that no one can penetrate. You think you're completely dead inside.

But then you walk by a freshly painted white house with an expansive green lawn. Something makes you stop—it's the gentle sounds of another creature, coming from an upstairs window. You hear a voice that is so untouched by any tragedy or misfortune that it breaks your heart. Then the beautiful voice stops and you continue on your way, but everything is different now. You know you are still capable of feeling things.

JOHNNY

Detroit, Michigan
September 2, 2001

This was what I used to do. Each morning, I'd get up and walk around the neighborhood, asking if anyone had a funny story to tell me. You know, maybe a joke, a little amusing thing that had happened to them recently, whatever. I just like a good chuckle.

I would stop every creature I saw and say, "Do you know any funny stories?" After a while, I just used to say, "Got anything for me?" Boy, I used to get some good ones too. Sometimes after one of those, I'd say, "Got another one?" or "So what else?" and then I'd get another chuckle or two.

Once I approached some new guy in town and asked him to tell me something funny. He stared at me. I stared back and smiled my most winning smile. Sometimes you gotta let them know that you're a warm audience that isn't going anywhere. Finally, he scowled and told me I was a rude imbecile. He screamed that I had no right to expect others to entertain me if I wasn't willing to reciprocate in any way. I turned around and ran back home, and never again asked anyone for a chuckle.

So that's why I'm sitting here in this crappy yard, not out there where I used to have good times.

KIP

Larchmont, New York
September 22, 1999

I have things I need to think about—theories I am working on relating to the unfair balances of power in the universe. They involve complex questions of logic and philosophy and if I can prove what I think I can, I am going to really impact our society in a profound way.

This is why I need total peace and quiet, which is what I used to have before this stupid little creature moved in next door. Gretchen is always making some sort of ruckus—when she's outside, she's wreaking havoc with the birds and the squirrels. When she's inside, she's breaking things and getting yelled at. And God help us all—sometimes she bangs on some musical instrument.

I have theories I need to prove and she is preventing me from doing this important work. And what is even more upsetting is that sometimes she comes to the fence and accuses me of being obsessed with her, which I assure you I am not.

I just want her to move away so things can go back to how they were. Even now, when it is relatively calm, I can't really concentrate because I know at any moment that insipid ninny is going to make some kind of noise.

KING

Cleveland, Ohio
October 4, 2000

The illness I had is something which I would prefer not to discuss. Suffice it to say, it was vile and I wouldn't wish it on anyone. I tried to keep it to myself for as long as I could. I don't like to be a bother. But eventually, they noticed and I was taken to a facility where I had to spend the night.

I couldn't sleep. I was in pain and my body was expelling horribly gross things. I looked over and saw that another creature was awake. Her name was Ruby and she was staying there for some minor reason. She stayed up with me all night. In the morning, when no one was looking, we got a chance to make love. It was the most beautiful experience of my life. I think part of the reason was that there I was at my most physically repulsive and yet this creature was still drawn to me.

We both went home and never saw each other again. I want to think that we shared a brief, but truly spiritual, connection, but sometimes I worry that it was simply a matter of Ruby being one of those creatures who has a deviant attraction to old sick guys.

ZEPPO
Meriden, Connecticut
June 30, 2000

I was out in the front yard fussing with some weeds one night when I heard some terrible screams coming from down at the end of the block. I thought they would stop, but they didn't. They just kept going. The voice sounded familiar. I gasped. It belonged to my friend Mitzi, who lived down there. It sounded as if she was being clawed to death.

I just stood there and listened to it happen. I happened to look across the street and saw my neighbor Sylvester listening. I turned and saw that my friend Coco was at the window of the house next door. I think about eight or nine of us were all listening as Mitzi's screams got worse and worse. And yet none of us did anything to help. We were all too scared to get involved.

Mitzi was found dead the next day. Sometimes I don't know how the rest of us go on.

PEACHES
Great Neck, New York
April 17, 1998

It's horrible when you find out what people say about you behind your back. I was out one day breaking in my freshly clipped nails when I overheard an old biddy named Flossie say to her friend that I was a complete fraud.

I went home and tried to take a nap, but I kept hearing Flossie's words in my head. I've always wanted everyone to think of me as a lovable, sweet guy, although deep down, I know I am mean-spirited and petty. Flossie had seen through my act. I started to wonder if everyone in the community could see through me.

I have never confronted Flossie on what she meant. I still smile and nod hello when I see her. But because of her, I am now in a constant state of fear and panic. I am wildly skittish, always wondering who will be the next creature to see through to the darkest part of me. I think I may even be developing a heart condition.

RED

South Orange, New Jersey
February 27, 2000

I was at a point in my life where I had all this crap I needed to deal with—stuff with my mother, all my old mates, my offspring. I would sit at home at night and my head would pound as I thought about these things, until one time when I couldn't take it anymore and I bolted up and went out and hit the streets. A few minutes later, I found myself in an alley having sex with a stranger. And during those frenzied moments, I forgot about anything else in my life.

Soon, I was hitting the alleys every night. As the sun went down, I would be giddy with anticipation. When I went home each dawn, I would be tired but exhilarated by the memories of that evening's random furtive couplings.

Then one night, I had sex with my seventh partner of the evening and got up to go home. She then said she wasn't going to let me leave her—I was all she had. I looked in her eyes and realized she was horribly mentally unstable, probably one of those cases you hear about who were thrown in drying machines at an early age. I edged away from her, but then suddenly she started screaming obscenities and scratched and bit me all over. She almost tore my ear off before I was able to get away from her.

As the sun came up that morning, I lay in a gutter bleeding profusely. I knew I had come very close to being killed. That was the wake-up call I needed to go home and begin putting the shattered pieces of my life back together.

PHILLIE
Williamsburg, New York
October 27, 2001

E ver since I can remember, I have had an irrational fear of being snickered at. I would walk down the street, then quickly turn to see if anyone was snickering at me even though I wasn't doing anything that would cause snickering.

As I got older, I learned that this neurosis signified a deeper problem, that of not accepting myself, but this did not make it go away. In fact, it got worse, to the degree that I stopped leaving the house altogether. I still turned around all day to see if anyone was snickering, but now at least I did it privately.

Then Shakti came to live here. She was very spiritual and sensed I had deep emotional wounds. She put her paws over different parts of my body in an effort to cleanse my aura.

Not only did I stop worrying about snickering, but after a few weeks of Shakti's therapeutic efforts, I was able to go outside for the first time in years. The fresh air was a tonic. The smell of the flowers on the front lawn was invigorating. Shakti watched me from the porch. She is a big believer in the healing powers of nature. I ran back in after a few moments, but I know I will go back out again at some point.

Because of Shakti, I have confronted my fears and learned that I have a strength that I didn't know I possessed.

MOO-MOO
Summit, New Jersey
December 11, 2000

Some of us can have everything, yet still have a hole inside, always feeling as if something is missing. I had a nice home, a loving mate, and wonderful offspring, but I felt restless and unfulfilled. Ava sensed this existed in me when she moved into the neighborhood and so she lured me into a tempestuous affair.

I've never met a creature like Ava. She's got this purr that could arouse a corpse. And she can knead you into a frenzy. We used to go at it for hours, waking up everyone who was in a two-block vicinity. Late one night, Ava asked if I loved her enough to kill another creature for her. She explained that he had lived in her old town and was mad at her for some toy swap that had gone wrong. Now he had moved nearby and was making threats against her life. She cried, and even though I didn't quite believe her story, I said I would do whatever she wanted me to.

We made it look like a car ran over him. A few months later, Ava asked me to kill someone else. I put up a fuss, but in the end I did it. I now kill for her almost every weekend, leading a dark and depraved secret life that can't be good for me.

YEATS

Westfield, New Jersey
June 10, 1998

I suffer from low self-esteem and I overcompensate by sometimes being too aggressive. Because of this, I have always been unhappy due to bad relationships or unhealthy living situations or just fights with various members of the community. Someone saw the pain I was in and suggested I go to Lester.

Lester is unbelievably brilliant and charismatic. I have never met anyone like him. His teachings incorporate various techniques that help you to get rid of your emotional baggage and move forward to become the best creature you can be.

All of us who study with Lester are devoted to making his life easier. We bring him food, we see that he has nice things to play with. Some of the younger ones sleep with him.

I am now much happier than I have ever been before. Everyone says that I am letting Lester run my life, but I don't listen to them. If I didn't have Lester, I know that I surely would have killed myself by now.

ORANGINA
Stamford, Connecticut
July 22, 1997

It seems so stupid now, but I ran away from home when I was young after some little territorial pissing incident. I lived life on the streets and got into some really bad scenes. Then I met Wolfie, a former runaway himself who took in misguided youths. He listened to me and treated me like a peer. I got my shit together and settled down in a nice home.

It's all because of Wolfie that I now counsel runaways myself. I suggest various ways they can make a life off the street—whether it is in going back to confront whatever they ran away from or in starting somewhere new like I did.

Wolfie taught me that we should all devote ourselves to a life of service, what he considered the only true path to inner peace. All around me I see sad and bored creatures who aimlessly stare and sleep all day. I wish they knew how much satisfaction they could get if only they would reach out, but whenever I try to tell them this, they yawn and walk away.

FRANCIS
Levittown, New York
March 4, 1998

I come from a small town in Georgia where all any of us did was sit on our front porches and gossip about everyone else who was also just sitting on their front porches. Nothing ever really happened, but we didn't care because we didn't have anything to compare it to.

Then Tex blew into town and all us ladies got real riled up, let me tell you. He was a fine-looking specimen with a mighty virile scent. The others threw themselves at him, but my mama taught me better. I wouldn't even sniff in his direction. And it didn't take long before he started coming to call on me. One night, he told me he was going to leave town and asked if I wanted to go with him. I was so scared to death that I was practically shaking, but I said yes.

Tex has shown me so much. We've been across this fine country four times now. 'Course we have our share of problems, like most folks do—I'll never get used to how his saliva gets everywhere. But mostly we get along real good and things are always interesting. Next week, Tex is going to take me somewhere to swim with the dolphins. I can't wait even though it sounds dangerous and I don't really take to water.

PETUNIA

Santa Fe, New Mexico
January 1, 1998

Dulcy is the dullest creature on the planet. She lives with me and I want to kill her.

She never just goes about her day. Instead, she informs me of what she is thinking about doing. For instance, instead of just jumping off a chair and going into the next room, she debates over whether she should or not. Then when she finally goes to the new place, she compares it to the old place. Sometimes it is better and sometimes it is worse, but it is never interesting.

She never defecates without first letting me know that she is planning to defecate. She details why she is going to defecate and what she expects to get out of defecating. After she defecates, a full report of the actual activities is made.

This is a very small apartment. I am never out of her sight. I have been on edge lately. Each dreadful detail of Dulcy's life is tearing away at what little sanity I have left.

FRANÇOIS
New York, New York
July 29, 2000

I don't know why Norm turned into a monster but he did and he's my offspring, so of course everyone thinks it's all my fault. I should have been a better parent. I shouldn't have spoiled him.

Maybe they're right. But he was so cute, and he was my first. I couldn't deny him anything. No one could. Everyone wanted to please him.

Maybe that's where he learned to use people for his own nefarious purposes, humiliating them and ruining their lives before moving on to his next victim. Or maybe he was just born heartless and perverse. Did you ever think of that?

Since Norm, I no longer have any peace. I simply go around and around in my head, wondering how someone made of pure evil could have come from me. I even wonder if I somehow mated with the devil, but that seems farfetched.

HILDEGARDE
Des Moines, Iowa
May 14, 1997

There were sixteen of us living in a small cabin in the Blue Ridge Mountains. Our family didn't have much, but we had a lot of love. I couldn't wait to get out of there.

I never knew how I would leave or what I would leave for. Then one day, a film crew came to the nearest town. I sat on a roof and watched them shoot a scene. There were all these trailers and lights and a big crowd and in the middle of it all was a beautiful creature that I recognized from things on television. She looked much tinier in real life. Everyone fussed over her and treated her like she was special.

I went to see them film every day and when they left, I was forlorn. A week later, I started walking toward Hollywood so I could be a star, just like the creature in the movie. It took me forever, but I got here. At first, I was ecstatic. But then the reality set in—I had no idea what to do next.

It's been years and I still haven't been discovered. I don't even have a crappy agent. Sometimes I get eaten up by jealousy when I see the no-talents who are working. I'm just as good as they are. Why did they get a break and not me?

I try to have a positive attitude and tell myself it will happen for me someday, but you meet a lot of creeps here. They prey on your insecurities and make you promises that never come true.

TILLIE

Hollywood, California
November 29, 2000

B oris and I lived in the same house for many years. I never really cared for him that much—he was always sprawled all over the place, constantly shedding, and had very unpleasant eating habits. At first, I tried to get him to behave in a more civilized manner, but when that failed, I simply kept my distance. From that point on, most of our communications were regarding household matters.

Boris liked to stupidly eat rich foods, so, of course, he was often violently ill. As such, he would get all the attention and special treatment. As the years passed, I think I began to resent him greatly.

Then one day Boris was struck down with influenza and taken away. They didn't know if he would come back. I was elated.

A short time later, I was told he was put to sleep. Now I find myself missing him. I wake up crying in the middle of the night. I don't understand whether I am romanticizing Boris or whether I am genuinely affected by his loss.

LADY
Fort Lee, New Jersey
April 3, 1999

I was a mere slip of a thing when they brought me here to the Vandertuckington estate to be mated with a creature named Alfred. We drove through elaborate gates and up a long, winding driveway. When this enormous house came into view, my fur stood on end but I had no idea why.

My first dinner here, in a kitchen pantry the likes of which I had never seen before, I met Alfred and his family, who had lived in this house for generations. Alfred was very polite, almost too much so. Alfred's mother scared me because she seemed like a zombie. Everyone explained that she was just quiet, but that didn't account for the weird look in her eyes.

I couldn't sleep that night. I heard noises—they said it was just the sounds of the ocean far below the cliffs we were on. But I had my doubts. I continued to hear these eerie sounds night after night and was sure this place was haunted.

One night I couldn't take it anymore and got up and wandered toward the noises. I went to the basement where I finally discovered the truth of this house with many secrets. Alfred and his brothers and sisters perform twisted and perverse acts all night long among themselves and sometimes with locals.

I tried to leave Alfred once, but he wouldn't let me. Instead I am forced to stay here and pretend that nothing is wrong. So I just sit here quietly, slowly turning into Alfred's mother.

SHELLEY

Bar Harbor, Maine
January 21, 1998

Don't be fooled by this charming little beach town. It's always the sunniest spots that have the darkest underbellies. And believe me, I know underbellies. You see, I'm a retired investigator for some of the creatures around here.

A couple of years ago, a stranger limped into my driveway and told me he had been attacked because someone wanted his beanbag toy. As the poor fellow took his final gasp, he talked not of his mate nor of that big creature up above. Instead, he spoke of how wondrous his precious beanbag was. He was about to tell me where it was hidden, but then he passed.

Whether it was to avenge the poor guy or because my curiosity was piqued, I knew I had to track down this beanbag. After a few dead ends, a shady character downtown said he might have some information for me. But when I went to meet him, all I found was a pool of blood, a pile of fur, and a couple of smudgy paw prints. Another poor goner had died because of this damn beanbag.

I have been on the hunt for it now for years. Some have told me that they think I am crazy and that this beanbag may not even exist, but I know that it does and someday, when I get my hands on it, I will have all that I have ever wanted.

THOMAS
San Diego, California
October 6, 1998

It happened over a decade ago. I saw an acquaintance named Dinah and went over to say hello. Before I could get a word out, she screamed that I was the most filthy beast she knew and called me other names and told me to get away from her.

I ran off and somehow ended up in the woods. I cried for quite some time, then happened to see my reflection in a stream. She was right—I was a filthy beast. I was obviously so disgusting that I should be exiled from society. So for the next ten years, I rarely ventured from the woods, mostly living on nuts and berries, and only very occasionally saw another creature.

Then in a freakish twist of fate, I happened upon Dinah on a deserted road outside town. She didn't remember me. I told her who I was and what she had said. At first she didn't recall the incident, then it hit her. I told her how her words had affected me. She was confused—she said she had just shouted at me because someone had dumped her and she wanted to be alone. And here I had taken it personally. I can't believe how stupid I have been.

CECIL
Port Washington, New York
August 1, 2000

You can't trust them—not one single one of them. I fell in love with Leonardo because I thought he was different than all the rest. But now I am sure that the lying bastard is cheating on me.

No, I don't have any actual proof, but I don't need it. Any idiot could see how he looks at other creatures hungrily, especially the slutty, trashy-looking ones. And his denials are so hollow. Oh please, don't tell me it's all in my head because it's not.

I follow him now, all the time. He's clever. He hasn't slipped up yet. But someday he'll make a mistake and I'll catch him with one of his little whores. I can't wait for that day. I'm going to scratch her eyes out and sink my teeth into her tail.

Sometimes Leonardo tells me I need to get help, and that's when I really go nuts—I shake tables and stand under them so things will fall on top of me and I will be maimed and so then maybe he will love me more and not want to cheat on me.

I swear, someday something really bad is going to happen because of Leonardo and his little chippies and it is no one's fault but his own.

HAGGIE
Van Nuys, California
October 14, 1998

A lustful stare, a sly glance—those are your constant companions when you're young and you're hot and you're strutting your stuff down the street.

Then you reach a certain age where they stop looking at you. You've gotten chubby, your fur is matted in places it never used to get matted. You have infections in your eyes that won't go away no matter what you do to take care of them.

The funny thing is, you still feel hot inside. Only now it's a delusion. And you spend all your time walking around with your tail in the air, hoping someone will look at you like they used to. But they don't. Then you start to hate yourself for being superficial and wonder if you were always that way and that's why you were never able to have any real sort of meaningful relationship.

A couple of months ago, I ran into George, one of the guys from the old neighborhood. He went on and on about how I hadn't changed a bit. I started feeling as if maybe I hadn't lost it.

I've been hanging out a lot with George now and I feel like myself again. I notice he constantly bumps into things. Of course it's occurred to me that he is blind, but I'd prefer to think that he is just unbelievably uncoordinated.

GIGI
Metuchen, New Jersey
March 24, 2001

I t's very unsettling when someone just disappears. You hope that maybe he or she met the love of their life and ran away. But that's never the case. Usually, they've been run over or drowned or have fallen victim to some other terrible fate.

Everyone was very upset when Peppermint vanished. She was so gentle and sweet—somehow that made it more tragic. All we talked about was what could have happened to her. Gradually we moved on with our lives, although every now and then someone would offer up some new theory as to her possible sad fate.

Then one day, months later, someone heard cries for help coming from a toolshed on a large property. It was Peppermint, who was stuck in a crawl space. She had subsisted on insects and water from a leaky pipe, and had recited affirmations all day long to keep from going mad. We all helped dig her out, and she returned to civilization remarkably unscathed by her experience.

Now when I see Peppermint, she fills me with awe. I wish I had just one ounce of her courage and fortitude. Sometimes I think I may be in love with her, but I am not sure.

ARIEL
Bernardsville, New Jersey
May 19, 1997

Those of us that grew up in homes where we weren't really wanted tend to have a hard time making friends. We spend a lot of time by ourselves and often become maladjusted.

This would have happened to me were it not for an old creature named Tabitha who lived down the street from me. Every now and then, she would ask me to help her in some way. She would give me little treats and tell me that I was special. Once she whispered in my ear that she knew I was destined for greatness in some way.

Tabitha's belief in me gave me the strength to face the many horrible things that happened to me later. Even at my lowest moments, there was a part of me that knew I would be able to triumph. She was the one who did this for me.

Later I found out that Tabitha told all the little creatures in the neighborhood the exact same thing. For a while, I was sad about this, but then I decided it didn't bother me. After all, it worked—so what if she didn't really mean it? And besides, maybe she felt that way about all of us. Maybe we're all destined for greatness, even those of us who aren't.

ANNA BANANA
Santa Rosa, California
October 28, 1998

At the beginning, Stan and I were very happy and in love, but then he started acting strangely.

His first request was that I roll around in a certain way. He was very specific. I was to start out on my right and always move to my left. It seemed harmless, so I agreed.

Then he asked me to run in a more graceful manner. He trained me to make small, delicate movements. It was difficult because my natural tendency is to lope, but I learned how to run the way Stan wanted me to.

The requests turned into demands. I had to chew my food in tinier bites, stretch precisely the way he wanted me to, jump off furniture at the angle he liked best.

I didn't understand why he cared so much about these things until we were making love and he called out the name of his first mate, Brittie. I realized he was trying to turn me into her.

Now I don't know what to do. I want to stay with Stan because I love him, but I want him to love me for who I am, not for being a robotic imitation of Brittie.

CHERIE
Irvington, New Jersey
June 15, 2000

We smelled the fire before we saw it. My best friend, Jack, and I were on our way back to the block where we both lived. Then we heard the fire engines. As we turned the corner, we saw that it was Jack's house on fire. Jack started to cry. I had never seen him like that. I was embarrassed and didn't know what to do.

Well, the fire destroyed the place. Everyone and everything Jack had was gone. He ended up starting a completely new life three doors down. And the funny part is, he's doing better than he ever was before. Jack used to be scared of unfamiliar things, but now he has been forced to try different food and nap in new places. Each day he can't wait to tell me about something he saw or did the night before for the first time.

This fire took years off him. He is much more vibrant than he used to be. I wish I were like Jack. I look around at where I live and who I live with and then I think, I'm suffocating. I want to set this place on fire.

FARNSWORTH
Shaker Heights, Ohio
January 31, 1997

One afternoon a stranger followed me as I was walking home. One thing led to another and I found myself back at his place, which was in a neighborhood that was unfamiliar to me.

He walked me back to a garage that was falling apart. When I reached the entrance, I suddenly didn't feel right. I turned around to leave, but he pushed me in and then sat on me and hypnotized me into never leaving this garage.

I know this story sounds insane, but it is a hundred percent true. My captor has big, dark eyes and he can make anyone do what he wants them to. So now I am a prisoner and even if you were to tell me that you could take me out of here and return me home safely, I wouldn't take you up on it because of the enormity of the hypnotic spell I am under.

I used to hate my captor, but now I don't mind him. I even think he is sweet sometimes. Of course it is confusing as to whether I have genuine feelings for him, or whether I have just been warped by being held prisoner in this mildewy place.

RAINDROP

Nutley, New Jersey
November 12, 2001

Look around me at this lovely yard, this house, my bountiful bowl of food in the kitchen. Others ask me how I came to have so much. I tell them it was all because of my friend Carol.

She told me that intention is everything. If you exude warmth and love, then unbelievable riches will accrue. It's a simple concept— I have no idea why everyone doesn't embrace it.

You see how magnetic and charming I am. You want to make me happy. I create this desire in you and all who come in contact with me.

Carol had the secret to ultimate fulfillment and she gave it to me and now I give it to you. What will you do with it?

VICTOR

Nyack, New York
April 16, 1999

I don't know her name. I call her Pretty. I noticed her the first day I moved to this house. She was sitting on the shelf in a back bedroom upstairs. She never moves from the spot. She is made out of glass. Next to her are some ugly pieces, but I don't even see them, not really.

I visit her often. I imagine conversations with her. It's odd, but in a way, she has the best sense of humor of anyone I have ever met. No one makes me laugh like she does.

Every now and then my feelings are so strong for her that I don't know how to handle it. I want to knock her off the shelf. After a while I get ahold of myself and the feeling passes.

On some level, I know this is not healthy. But at the same time, Pretty makes me happy like no one else does. She is perfect.

LUIS
Narragansett, Rhode Island
June 1, 2000

No one meant for anything bad to happen. There were five of us playing in an abandoned factory. We were just having some vaguely homoerotic competitions, then Luthor accidentally killed a frail creature named Moonie.

We covered up his body and all went back to our respective homes. I have been trying to stay away from the others, but we run into each other here and there and guiltily look away.

I am scared of Luthor. He keeps saying he knows one of us is going to crack, and if we do, he is going to come after us.

JOHNSON
Newark, New Jersey
December 2, 1998

Hunter used to talk about leaving his mate. He said as soon as she got over her bout with parasites, we would run off together. But then they discovered she had crippling arthritis and he never again said anything about us having a real future. Instead, I have to settle for a few stolen moments here and there when he can get away from that witch.

I hate myself for being someone's mistress. I rarely go out and do anything because I never know when Hunter will show up. When I hear him at the door, I jump up, frenziedly, with joy. When he leaves, I rip up the furniture and then overeat and throw up.

I suppose there have been others who were interested in me, but I never pursued it. My best friend tells me I am scared of true intimacy, but she's just jealous of what Hunter and I have.

When a few weeks go by and I haven't seen Hunter, I get a really bad case of the nerves and can't focus on anything. Invariably, he turns up and I make a big scene and tell him it's over between us. But we both know that it isn't.

STRAWBERRY

Philadelphia, Pennsylvania
October 27, 2000

W e called him Stinky. I don't even remember what his real name was. He had an ugly birthmark under his left ear. We used to make fun of him and beat him up because he had a high voice. After I moved away from the small town we lived in, I never thought about Stinky much, although to be honest, when I did think about what we did to him, I felt bad.

A year ago, I saw Stinky on the street, here in the city. I called out to him. He looked straight at me and walked away. My friend asked me why I was calling that creature "Stinky." I said that was his name and told her how I grew up with him. She said I must be mistaken. His name was Prince Romenescu, and he was from Budapest. She said he most certainly did not have a high voice—he had a low, masculine growl that was highly erotic. But I saw that birthmark. I don't know how Stinky reinvented himself, but he did.

It gives me a kick now when I see Stinky with his big-shot fancy-pants friends. He makes me believe that anything is possible.

EVELYN
Chicago, Illinois
April 29, 1998

You are like everyone else. You feel bad for me because I live on the streets. But my heart beats faster than yours does and I have known greater joy and fear and love and hate. I would kill myself if I had to live in some depressing little suburban home, at the mercy of others all day and night.

I met my lover Glitter several years ago and we have incredible sex. She and I tried having an exclusive relationship, but neither of us is the type. So sometimes we go for months without seeing each other, each of us prowling different parts of town.

But then one of us will send word to the other to meet at a designated parking structure and then we'll have a wild weekend of debauchery together. Glitter is really my best friend. I know if I'm in a pinch, she'll be there for me. And vice versa. I don't need anything or anyone else because I know I have Glitter.

MISS PAMELA
Jersey City, New Jersey
February 6, 2001

My friend Misty woke up one afternoon with a terrible itch on the side of her head, just below her ears. She rubbed this spot against furniture the whole rest of the day. Every time she took a nap, she thought she would wake up and the itch would be gone. But it never was. This went on for weeks.

Various remedies were tried, but none worked. Misty had a permanent itch, and she lived with it for years and years.

There were times when I would be troubled by a neighboring creature or I would have problems with my mate and I would feel sorry for myself. But in talking to Misty and watching her rub her head against whatever was handy, I would suddenly find myself able to look past my own petty concerns.

On the evening Misty passed, she was still rubbing away just as vigorously as the first day she got the itch. She had lived the vast majority of her life with a terrible itch. But the itch never got her down or kept her from doing anything. Many would have let the itch win, but she didn't.

SYLVIO
Morristown, New Jersey
July 21, 1999

Did you notice that incredible house on the corner with the big front yard and fragrant bushes? That was supposed to be mine, but I was done out of it by this jerk named Scruffy.

The details aren't important. But suffice it to say, he took my spot in the good place, and I ended up here in this dump. And yes, I haven't starved and I have always had shelter over my head. But it's not like it should've been.

Some days, all I think about is Scruffy. I eat my little food and wonder, is Scruffy eating something moister? I go to defecate and think, is Scruffy defecating somewhere nicer? I try to nap, but I can't—I am tortured by the idea that Scruffy is lying on a cushion far superior in every way to the one I have.

TADPOLE
Highland Park, Illinois
March 29, 1997

Someone named Hubert came up to me at a gathering and told me about a strange nightmare he had had. It involved giant rodents roaming around, feasting on creatures such as myself. The way Hubert described the dream, it was very vivid and scary.

A few days later, I woke with a start—I was having the dream that Hubert had. I continued to have it the following day and the day after. Now I can't get rid of the nightmare Hubert gave me. Everyone tells me I look as if I am being tortured when I am napping.

Even though I sleep, I never feel rested. Because I am so tired, I fall down a lot. I get all sorts of advice—don't use my pillows for anything but napping, somehow find a way to get my paws on warm milk before I go to sleep—but nothing works.

I suppose I shall pass away someday from exhaustion due to Hubert's nightmare.

BROWNIE

Monsey, New York
September 1, 2001

According to my neighbor Rosemary, everything I do is wrong. When I kill birds, she tells me that I am too sloppy and shouldn't make such a needless mess. She watches me as I clean myself and says the better way would be to wipe my tongue off periodically so I don't spread the germs around. Rosemary even has the nerve to criticize my frolicking. Her exact terminology was that I "land with a thud that is not very attractive."

I have told Rosemary over and over again that she can do things her way and I can do things mine, but she doesn't listen. I know she is old, and maybe she is lonely, but I still lose my patience with her. She's over there right now, holding her tongue. I know she's thinking I am not being interviewed the way she would be interviewed and it is all she can do not to butt in.

BUMPERS

Peapack, New Jersey
April 11, 2000

I was up on a ledge, fourteen stories high. I was racing because I was late for a romantic assignation.

I turned a corner and found myself behind a slow creature. I pushed him off the ledge so I could get by.

The creature died, the community found out about it, and now I am permanently shunned.

GILLIGAN
Trenton, New Jersey
May 30, 2001

It was one of those amazing nights where you're digging through garbage finding one piece of delicious food after another. I was with my pal Bud and as we stuffed ourselves, we became giddy with delight.

Then Bud cut himself on a can and started bleeding profusely. I got scared, thinking he might die. But the bleeding eventually stopped, and we started for home as the sun began to rise.

I watched Bud limp and told him how sorry I was he got hurt. He smiled and said he didn't mind. It was all part of the experience of the night. He wanted the entire experience—both the good and the bad parts. That was the only way you ever really knew you experienced something fully.

For some reason, those words really resonated with me and permanently adjusted my perceptions quite markedly.

TURK

New Haven, Connecticut
July 22, 2001

This is a story about true bravery. I grew up in a home with thirty-six others. Everyone got along okay except for Frankie, who was a sadist. He delighted in torturing everyone, but in particular he picked on the smallest one of us, Buttercup.

One hot summer day, Frankie was even meaner than usual, singling out Buttercup in particular. When Frankie left the room, we all bitched about him, as we usually did. But this time, Buttercup didn't just moan about his fate. He went over to Frankie's favorite pillow and puked on it. We were all nervous, but elated by this small but daring act of rebellion.

A short time later, Frankie came back and sat in the puke. We laughed. Frankie made a face, smelled what he was sitting in, and immediately figured out what had happened. He viciously beat up Buttercup, who didn't care in the least.

This tiny gesture of revolt was the first step in a campaign that ended in Frankie's expulsion from the home. Buttercup taught all of us something important about how to make a difference.

CRICKET

Massapequa, New York
November 11, 1999

It seems like I spent forever trying to meet someone who would love me and who I could love too.

I tried everything you could possibly think of—I worked on myself constantly. I battled the inner demons from my youth that were making me participate in the old self-destructive patterns of behavior. I took medication. I changed my physical appearance. And I am telling you, nothing worked.

Then Clarissa came into my life unexpectedly one day when she dropped out of a tree, literally. She and I have been inseparable ever since. I am gloriously happy. I feel Clarissa and I are one.

And it happened without my having anything to do with it, which just goes to show you.

TICK-TOCK

Spring Lake, New Jersey
June 26, 2001

ABOUT THE AUTHOR

Bruce Eric Kaplan has contributed more than four hundred cartoons to *The New Yorker,* many of which were collected in his first book, *No One You Know.* He lives in Los Angeles, where he has written for such television shows as *Seinfeld* and *Six Feet Under.*